WITH AENEAS

IN A TIME

OF PLAGUE

With AENEAS
IN A TIME
OF PLAGUE

CHRISTOPHER BURSK

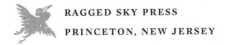

RAGGED SKY PRESS
PRINCETON, NEW JERSEY

Published by Ragged Sky Press
270 Griggs Drive, Princeton, NJ 08540
www.raggedsky.com

Library of Congress Control Number: 2021936255

ISBN: 978-1-933974-42-2

Cover and book design: Jean Foos
Cover art: Deborah Kahn, *Green Animal with Figures*, 2014, oil on canvas

Printed in the United States of America

First Edition

iam pectore toto
accipio et comitem casus complector in omnis.
Nulla meis sine te quaereretur gloria rebus:
seu pacem seu bella geram, tibi maxima rerum
verborumque fides.
—Vergil, *Aeneid,* Book IX

For Rick Churchill and Fred Blair

❧ ❧ ❧

Cessi, et sublato montes genitore petivi
—Vergil, *Aeneid,* Book II

For Edward Collins Bursk

❧ ❧ ❧

And lo! from opening clouds, I saw emerge
The loveliest moon, that ever silver'd o'er
—John Keats, *Endymion,* Book I

**For Mary Ann and for our children and grandchildren
And for my brothers**

CONTENTS

III. Studying the Classics at Fifteen

IV. Reading the *Aeneid* at Seventy-six

I. CESSI, ET SUBLATO

MONTES GENITORE PETIVI

"Enough," our father said and shut the Aeneid
so conclusively my brother and I were not sure
he'd ever open it again.

At the Cave of the Sibyl of Cumae

non ulla laborum,
o virgo, nova mi facies inopinave surgit;
omnia praecepi atque animo mecum ante peregi.
Unum oro: quando hic inferni ianua regis
dicitur et tenebrosa palus Acheronte refuso,
ire ad conspectum cari genitoris
　　　　　　　　—*Aeneid,* Book VI, Seamus Heaney, tr.

When I was six, I told myself
if I could just survive first grade
I could probably survive anything.

Then my dog ran back into the yard
with my friend's cat in its mouth
and the cat felt like a package damaged in the mail
and I didn't know what to do
with my hands afterwards.

When I visited my mother in the hospital
her face had turned the white of store-bought lilies
just before they wilt,
her lips quivering as if the electricity was still inside her
looking for a way out.

Nothing could be worse than this,
I told myself at eighteen, letting the car idle
and wishing I wasn't who I was: a boy
so desperate to catch a glimpse of his ex-girlfriend
he drives by her house every night.

And then I was a father humming
my ten-month-old daughter to sleep
the night before her operation.
I sang so softly I could barely hear the words myself.

If only I could be that Aeneas
who proclaims in Book VI of the *Aeneid,*
No ordeal, O Sibyl, no new test can dismay me,
for I have fore-seen and fore-suffered all.
But I have read Book VII
and know what comes next.

Nisus & Euryalus

"Me! Me!" (he cried) "turn all your swords alone
On me—the fact confessed, the fault my own.
He neither could nor durst, the guiltless youth—
Ye moon and stars, bear witness to the truth,
His only crime (if friendship can offend)
Is too much love to his unhappy friend."
                    —*Aeneid*, Book IX, John Dryden, tr.

Age 17, lines 229–231

How many kids besides me skimmed	the *Aeneid*	in bed
for ill-fated lads in linen skirts dyed purple?	Pulchior	Ascanius's
last words to pulchior Euryalus meant	for me.	*Be wholly*
mine. Take full possession of my soul.	Peach-fuzzed	Trojan lads
proved even more adorable when garbed	in Latin.	Was I perhaps
the only boy in the land masturbating	to Vergil	in the original?

Age 25, lines 258–259

How did Dryden know I needed those lines right	then	waiting
to be arrested? In our war we had no Aeneas, just	Richard	Milhous
Nixon and I, a new father, couldn't afford to	die	for my country
but I didn't want my son's godfather to die either,	so I lay down	on the street
and let men hurt me on the 5 o'clock news. They	had clubs	and so used them.
They had tear gas. And I? I had Vergil and rage	and guilt	and used them.

Age 40, lines 447–448

It's dangerous to read the *Aeneid* in middle age,	destiny then	more seductive
than Dido. You put your faith in heroes, and	for the sake	of your sons
stand in the rain, as if corruption might be washed	away.	Phalanxes
of police officers hurl towards you with no	intentions	of stopping.
They too believe in destiny, but have no more	use	for you
and your drenched comrades than they do	for the rain,	its manifestos.

Age 60, lines 506–508

Having slit the throat of a man strong enough to	wrestle Ajax	and win,
of course, Euryalus wanted bright swag, a souvenir	helmet	begging
to be lifted off one head onto his own. Vergil	makes us	watch
the boy cut down *like a white poppy, betrayed*	*by armor*	on which
the moon with full reflection plays. No better	teacher than	Publius Maximus:
If you're going to slit someone's throat, spurn	*all flashy*	*spoils.*

Age 78, lines 571–573

Now that plague is spreading its empire faster	than	the Romans
and I have grandsons earnest and lithe as Euryalus	and just	as susceptible
to time's brutal pleasures, I find myself	like Nisus	his body
thrown before the horses, shouting *Me, me,*	*adsum*	*qui feci,*
in me convertite ferrum Turn	*your swords*	*against me!*
Take your swords to me! Turn all your swords	*alone*	*upon me.*

A Prayer for Pallas

At vos, o superi, et divum tu maxime rector
Iuppiter, Arcadii, quaeso, miserescite regis
et patrias audite preces. Si numina vestra
incolumem Pallanta mihi, si fata reservant,
si visurus eum vivo et venturus in unum,
vitam oro, patior quemvis durare laborem.
                    —*Aeneid*, Book VIII, David Ferry, tr.

If by the will of the gods my son survive
And I live to meet him yet again,
There is no trouble I cannot endure.
And so the father entrusted Pallas
to Aeneas and the fates:
sexcentos illi dederat Populonia mater
expertos belli iuvenes, ast Ilva trecentos
insula inexhaustis Chalybum generosa metallis.
600 battle-hardened Populonian youth;
from Ilva's iron mines, 1000 bristling spears.

When I first typed these lines,
the plague had already claimed 240 in our county,
865 in our state,
77,212 nationwide
but now the virus is revising its figures
to over 507,269 in the country
our 45th president was trying to make great
again; 53,392 in the Italy
to which the son of Anchises voyaged
and where, having scraped Pallas off the battlefield—
that prayed-for son, that unlucky lad—

Aeneas made possible Rome and its Golden Age.
Today we gather six feet apart
as if muses have come down from Helicon:
Calliope, Clio, Thalia, Erato, Melete, Mneme,
Polyhymnia, Euterpe, each staking out her territory
before the house of a friend
so feverish and weak
we don't know what else to do but lift our voices
in song. We know music and poetry
will not save anyone, but we sing anyway.

The Plague in Early Spring

In these early weeks of the pandemic, landscaping
crews have been busy cutting away rotting branches.
—Philadelphia Inquirer, April 23, 2020

The first week in the first year of the plague,
when we told ourselves there was no plague,
the flowers were more than willing
to confirm our opinion.

The second week of the plague
we were careful to remind ourselves
we did not have any symptoms
and only the old and infirm had to worry,
and the trees offered themselves
as emblems of how perhaps even such culling was natural.

The fifth week of the plague
we flung open windows
and dared the virus to break into our houses,
some of us even tempted to embrace the fever
and get it over with.

The sixth week of the plague
we started hating tulips and daffodils
for flaunting themselves just outside our windows
as if there were no such thing as a plague.
And the trees?
What high and mighty airs they still put on!

Our children convince us now that they're dying
of boredom, glare at us
as if it's our fault that we were all born
a lower evolutionary organism susceptible to disease.
Whole families stand at the windows
and wait for something terrible to happen
to the oblivious lilies of the valley,
complacent gladioli.

Today we hate wren and chickadee most of all.
It's not just that they come and go
as they please. It's their melodies old as Homer we resent.

Nor are we fit to force our way across

—*Aeneid*, Book V, John Dryden, tr.

Because the first symptoms are a dry cough
I started coughing
three days ago
and because sore throat proves one of the early warning signs
I've kept swallowing
to see if my throat hurts
till now it does
and because chills often accompany the virus
I find myself shivering
so I run baths hot enough
to burn away the fever
though every time I take my temperature
it reads 97.7
so I suspect the thermometer
of lying and make everywhere I am a bed
and the cats lie down next to me
as if they know
I am dying though I show no signs of expiring
yet—except this
24-hour exhaustion, every cell in me tired
of what it knows
will be asked of it, every muscle clenching
for the onslaught. I keep closing my eyes
as I did as a child
when what I'd always feared would happen
happened and I knew,
seeing the ambulance drive away with my mother,
it was my fault
and so I kept taking naps
when I wasn't even sleepy
and then waking up
suddenly—as if to catch time off-guard.
I still shut my eyes
any moment I can
because so many of those I love are already sick

and I don't know why
I am not
and there's nothing I can do
to change that
and very little I can do to help anyone
and when I was a child
I wanted with all my heart to be the one
to suffer, and, at the same time, I must confess
I wanted, with all my heart,
not to suffer.

Easter Cancelled

What shall I do? Where go,
When I have cast this serpent-skin of woe?—
                    —Endymion, Book III

Who knows when or if
there will be school again?
There's no traffic anymore.
Cars
can go anywhere now and
get there on time
only there are not many
places to go.
The stores are shut
till further notice,
the theaters dark. Kids
watch so much television
it begins to feel like
punishment,
even a teenager can play
only so many video games
before he feels trapped
inside the screen.
The most loving families
tire
of Parcheesi and Yahtzee,
Monopoly and Scrabble.
Today the newspapers
publish instructions
for abused women:
Avoid any room that has furniture
with sharp edges.
Say as little of importance
as you can. It's Easter.
But the Lord
our God will have to rise
without us. On Passover
this year the Israelites must
escape Egypt
on their own. Though it's
only a pandemic,
we call it the plague
to confer on ourselves
at least the dignity of
suffering a biblical event
our great-grandkids will
study in history class.
What will we do
if and when the plague is over?
That's the game we play
at night:
we will rush to the malls
and buy everything
we have no real use for,
we will fill our grocery carts
with the earth's
new abundance,
we will bring our children
to Sunday school, every week, we will
touch strangers' faces,
we will kiss each other
on the lips
just because we can.

Pietà

—early 4th century, paint on wood

Jesus looks as if he'd already decided years before
not to demean his mouth
with anything as trivial as food,
and had by now grown thoroughly bored
with the hard, compromising work of being human:
the effort it takes to peel an apple or cut your toenails
or hold in your piss
when all you want to do is give in to one of many pleasures
available to the human body.

Is that a shudder on the Son of God's lips?
Or a smile? Pity
on Mary's face or disgust, given all that body fluid
her son's dripping on her, his uncooperative limbs
that refuse to gather in her lap,
her one hand tentative on our Lord and Savior's hip
as if she's trying to make up her mind
whether or not to let him drop away?
His head's flung so far back you can almost see an ocean wave
about to snap it off.
She cradles the Messiah
the way you might someone lifted out of the sea
too late to be saved.

Mary looks like a meadow
in whose folds you could fall asleep;
Jesus naked as water
his mother's trying to cup in her hand,
Go ahead, he seems to be saying
Crucify me.
Then try to comfort me the best you can.

For the Boy I Wanted, Fifty Years Ago, to Take to the Senior Prom

Quale manus addunt ebori decus, aut ubi flavo
Argentum Pariusve lapis circumdatur auro.
                                        —*Aeneid*, Book I

This week your throat has refused to swallow
any of your favorites we tempt it with—
black Bing cherries, Pemaquid oysters, minced papaya.
It's too difficult to nibble biscuits
softened in milk—your lips spurning
even rice pudding and the exotic purees
that pretend they're just as appetizing
as solid food—banana-pepper puree,
organic cilantro puree, green goddess puree.
It's one thing to ask you to be brave,
but to demand that of your salivary glands,
your esophagus too? Your tongue has enough trouble
chewing air into words.
Has your mouth concluded that it's time
to turn to higher matters?
And what of us? Who swarm around you
like a congregation of flies.
Like a family trying to persuade their wayward boy
not to set off on some cockeyed vision quest.
Like old lovers blocking the monastery door.
Like children begging for just one more page
in the story they don't want ever to end.
Even wasting away, you're as gorgeous
as Aeneas stepping out of the cloud
his mother had spun around him.
One more drink of water,
we plead. Just one more sip of water.

I Ask My Friends to Read *Endymion* with Me

O Moon! the oldest shades 'mong oldest trees
Feel palpitations when thou lookest in:
O Moon! old boughs lisp forth a holier din
The while they feel thine airy fellowship.
Thou dost bless everywhere, with silver lip
Kissing dead things to life.
　　　　　　　—John Keats, *Endymion*, Book III

No matter how often Keats spooned soup
to his brother's mouth, soothed his brow,
Tom's fever spiked, and so one more poet succumbed
to periphrasis, every apostrophe
an opportunity to digress, every prepositional phrase
a lush bower. In every noun garlanded
Adonis waking, every single simile porous,
the entire English language leaking
like a boat that refuses to be bailed
no matter how many times you dip your bucket down.
Slippery blisses, twinkling eyes
adjectives multiplying like paramecia,
swarming like Penelope's suitors,
greedy, insensitive flies,
adverbs licentiously cozying up to their verbs.
If Keats couldn't save one brother,
perhaps he could give birth to another: a milk-fed prince
of melancholy, a rural metaphysician,
and provide refuge for him in heroic couplets,
holding his breath
at each line's end as if not sure
he had the strength
to complete the rhyme.
Yes, Keats's lovesick shepherd's dedication
to his own pain seems willful, an old dependency
of wet dreams, iambs
fainting in each other's arms,
held captive by their own chastity.
There is not a fiercer hell than failure in a great object...
and there is no worse way to drown—
Some of us have buried our own brothers

and sisters and children. Some of our friends
have walked into the paths of cars
or died more methodically
with gun or gin or spent their last weeks clutching their ribs
as if they'd been knifed
but can't find where the blade broke skin,
and some of us still wake, convinced
the person who slept beside us every night for decades
is still beside us and some of us
even get out of bed and walk the halls, looking
for him or her. Only a few weeks ago
I kissed the closed eyes of a man
I'd loved since old enough
to know I'd love no one more
fervently than a tree loves every leaf.
And I don't know where else to seek comfort
right now but in these 31,151 words
struggling to hold what light
they can. In the midst of contagion
Keats calls forth cupids
to rub *their sleepy eyes with lazy wrists.*
Rise, Cupids! or we'll give the blue-bell pinch
To your dimpled arms. Once more
Sweet life begin! The poet sought his friend Bailey
and made him sit still for how summer *has talk'd*
Full soothingly to every nested finch.
Keats couldn't help himself,
one more anguished plea in lavish disguise.

Turning to Page 194 in the Very Same Copy of the *Aeneid* from Which My Father Read to My Brother, 9, and Me, 5

It was young Ascanius's first war.

Bring back my father, let me see him.
What can we fear when he's with us?

Father's return alone can save us—

Quaecumque mihi fortuna fidesque est,
in vestris pono gremiis: revocate parentem,
reddite conspectum; nihil illo triste recepto.

What I do not wish my children ever to think

though even now, gazing out the window
at a darkness that obliterates fathers and sons
I find my lips forming

Immo ego vos, cui sola salus genitore reducto

as if saying something in Latin might make it happen.

Thus was it in Latium—Translating Vergil Three Months into the Plague

Talia per Latium. Quae Laomedontius heros
cuncta videns magno curarum fluctuat aestu,
atque animum nunc huc celerem, nunc dividit illuc.
In partisque rapit varias perque omnia versat:
sicut aquae tremulum labris ubi lumen aenis
sole repercussum aut radiantis imagine lunae
omnia pervolitat late loca, imaque sub auras
erigitur summique ferit lacuaria tecti.
                    —*Aeneid,* Book VIII, David Ferry, tr.

When I was seven, I saw two men kill another man.
They were walking in snow
that came up to their waists.
The first man didn't think to turn around.
The second stabbed him
and when he wouldn't fall
the other man pushed him over.
I saw it all happen
on my closet door. There was too much blood
for it not to be real.

                    * * *

One night when I was twelve
and had just been given the top-floor corner room
now my brother had left home
I woke to find a man staring
in the window. He was a candle I couldn't blow out.
How could he stand there, three stories up,
without a ladder? Could enough hate
enable a person to do anything?
I didn't move a muscle
all night. Every time I stole a look
he was still glaring at me
as if there was nothing I could ever do
to make anyone forgive me.

***

Thus was it in Latium. And all the while
Laomedon's heir was going room to room
In his mind, this battle plan or that, this body count
Or that, try this door or another
As when the light chooses water shivering
With wind and then discards it for a brass bowl
That welcomes it just long enough for you to imagine
Dipping your hand in its rays. Window, perhaps
Door maybe, ceiling, wall, the sun slipping
From one object to another like a restless shopper.

***

Even stalwart Aeneas at times finds himself liable
to distraction. *Perhaps? Maybe?*
Even light, that heroic old Greek, can't seem to decide
sometimes—*Here*
or there?—*This object or that?*—
as if it makes all the difference
where it lands.

My Mother Places Stones in My Hand

Want to know the smaller stone's secret?
Put it in your mouth.
Try to crack it between your teeth like a seed,
she says in a voice I know
not to disobey. *Turn the larger stone over,*
find the gorge whose river
has abandoned it, the crater with a door
that can't be opened,
the winds restless in both stones,
the clouds that, not knowing which way to turn,
turn everywhere.
Then with her hand she closes my hand
over the stones,
and when I open my eyes

Bleu celeste, bleu d'azur, bleu barbeau, bleu bleut

I

It's been eight days, four hours,
and twenty-three minutes
since I took you by the ankles and lifted your obedient
body up on the bed just enough
to slip off your briefs. Someone had cared enough
to make absorbent underwear for men
cornflower blue, so I dressed you in a swath
of meadow and set you back
to the task at hand: sleeping
the sleep of the freshly diapered and powdered.

* * *

It's been a fortnight and a day
and an hour and five minutes
since the hospice nurse told your husband, *Soon,*
yes, very soon.

* * *

When you woke briefly from your coma
and looked up, surprised,
and said, *Kristofer, you are here!*
for the first time in my life
I actually liked my name.

* * *

Then your daughter whispered to you in French
not able to say goodbye to you
in a language she used for making appointments.
Then your son laid his hand on your shoulder
as if the two of you were teammates
about to play a difficult foe you'd beaten before.
Then Fred sat on the bed
as if it was a boat and, any minute, he'd have to start rowing
and I just stood there

like someone on shore, waving
at the boat by now too far out to recognize anyone.

* * *

31,760 minutes to be exact.

* * *

How to fill an afternoon?
That was our challenge
when we were eight and seven,
boys who hated football and loved crayons,
their infinite amount of options just for the color of sky.
Opening a brand-new box
was like being first to walk on just-fallen snow.

* * *

It's been 72 years, 4 months, 12 days, and 7 hours
since that afternoon
your mother, new to the neighborhood,
came for tea and brought you,
and when you refused to open your mouth
I dumped crayons on the floor
and they lay there like wounded soldiers
till finally we started drawing pictures
and sometimes I'd catch you looking
at the child plummeting through my azure sky
and sometimes I'd stop
to admire the boat you were making
sink into turquoise waves.
It was that rare time in America
when no one was dying
and Binney & Smith had just come up with more colors
and we had the whole afternoon to quarrel
over Cerulean or Azure
or Cobalt as if everything depended on choosing
the right crayon. At eight I thought
I'd spend my entire life with you,
on that floor, making the firmament
whatever *bleu* we wished it to be.

II. Vergil

at Bedtime

You'd think Priam's son being dismembered
before his father wouldn't make an ideal bedtime story,
though it did teach us never to breathe easy.

The Day Everything Changed

I do not remember the exact date,
but I won't forget the smell of rain still in the screen door
and the man on the other side
trying to catch his breath
as if he'd hurried here from a place very far away.
He had knocked three times
and then paused
and knocked more sharply three times again
shifting his weight from leg to leg
and reaching out
as if he had a package to deliver
though his hands held nothing.
He had a scar over his left eye
that seemed to have never healed.
When he lifted one palm to the screen door
I lifted mine
to his dimpled skin pressed hard
against the mesh, and then
he leaned his whole head against the door
till his face seemed made of many tiny rectangles.
I think of this day off and on.
It's one of those stories I tell my grandchildren
in the hopes of finally understanding it.
There was only wire between us
and such hurt in the man's eyes.
I learned, that day, the real meaning of the word
naked. Then he left,
though I don't remember him going away
any more than I might this leaf
or that leaf dropping from my favorite tree,
the one that every winter
I wasn't sure would ever bud again.
I have measured my life from this moment on
though I am not sure when it happened
or if it ever did.

Last Judgment of Hunefer

—Book of the Dead, ca. 1300–1290 BCE

Maybe death won't be so bad
if it means getting to hold the hand of a god
with the body of an athlete
and the head of a jackal.
That would be a far better way to spend the day
than being beat up at recess.
I start making myself sick right before school,
so I'll be home just in case
they come to take my mother away
again. She lets me borrow one of the books
she hasn't torn all the pages from.
It's my favorite, full of bare-chested men
with cryptic smiles.
By noon I have Anubis's strong, persuasive arms
around my waist, my heart weighed
by the goddess Maat. I yield
to the inscrutable, its rigorous
otherworldly demands.

Troy Sunk in Flames I Saw (Nor Could Prevent)

—Aeneid, Book II, John Dryden, tr.

Our father shut the book
he shouldn't have opened
any dark you uncover they'll beg
into it. Take away their mother

to busy their hands. I had a bed
when I was Dido. Drymas, I
of fire. Then Priam's son, I found
before Priam's eyes. Then Priam,
a funeral pyre. My brother

unpunished in the games he and
made us play. *Hold out your arm!*
he held another to his own arm.
enough to deserve
And, father, sometimes

like a trapdoor
for boys:
to drop
they'll find other ways

all flames
swallowed mouthfuls
myself speared
my throne
let no one go

Vergil
the match exhausted,
We had to hurt
to be Dardanians.
we did.

The Necropolis of Tarquinius

What are you boys doing? our father asked
though he really didn't want to know
why we had pickaxes in our hands.
We'd just discovered a new word—*necropolis*—
and now we wanted a city of the dead
of our own. But it was too hard digging life-size
trenches, so we settled for the flower garden
our mother wouldn't need anymore.
Once we'd finished our burial plots
we required bodies
to bury, so Timothy started embalming
the marionettes our mother used to let us play with
on rainy days: dainty king
and queen and the rest of the royal family
with their servants and musicians,
all conscripted to die with their ruler,
each placed in a sarcophagus
we'd molded out of what was left of our mother's
potter's clay. Before each lid hardened
Timothy carved winged monkeys for it
and harp-playing lions, pomegranates and eggs,
and we placed inside tiny tablets
on which we had inscribed hieroglyphs
for the dead to decode,
packed also miniature baskets of raisins and rice
in case anyone needed to eat
as well as read
in the underworld. We nestled under each prince's head
small pillows we'd stuffed
with pine needles; Timothy had read in a book
that the last sense to leave the body was smell.
And now it was time,
he said, to seal the tombs. We buried an entire nation
under brick, mud, then pebbles,
then earth rounded high enough
for us to find the tumuli again,
but no, Timothy said, we could not dig anyone back up.
This was it.
There was no question of resurrection.

Tantae molis erat Romanam condere gentem

Far too many sails to be
rigging tested, ships
yanked back
Deer to be slaughtered,
to be betrayed, Cyclopes
troops not only housed and
but given pep talks.
among one thousand men,
requiring innumerable
nouns and irregular verbs,
to be learned, so much
suffering.
never suspected
it would prove
reefed,
constantly
on course.
women
to be outwitted,
fed cakes,
Imagine all the squabbles
all of this
Latin
so much geography
gratuitous
My brother and I
how tedious
being a hero.

Atque ea diversa penitus dum parte geruntur

Irim de caelo misit Saturnia Iuno
audacem ad Turnum.
      —*Aeneid,* Book IX, Sarah Ruden, tr.

As a child, I thought my dad actually knew Aeolus
and Neptune, Juno and Iris,
not to mention Homer and Euripides, Cicero
and Ovid. I used to answer the door
imagining Sophocles on the other side

or I'd fall asleep, expecting Vergil
to put down the *Aeneid* and kiss me goodnight
as my father might have
if he hadn't found me so distasteful
compared to Ascanius and Pallas.

'Tene,' inquit 'miserande puer, cum laeta veniret,
invidit Fortuna mihi, ne regna videres
nostra neque ad sedes victor veherere paternas?'

I envied Ascanius lounging in Dido's lap
or eating cakes in Sicily
but I hated Pallas. How could I compete with a boy
of onyx eyes and snowy chest
and an open wound?
Not just a dutiful son but a pale and lovely one
and bravely dying.

Now the war master Mars gave strength and spirit
To the Latins, twisting sharp goads in their hearts,
While siccing Rout and black Fear on the Trojans.

The gods? Those astonishing contrivances
their rabid progeny, their viral incursions?

I thought if anyone could make them behave
it would be you, father.

Burning the Fleet

> *Struck with sight and seized with rage divine*
> *The matrons prosecute their mad design,*
> *They shriek aloud, they snatch with impious hands*
> *The food of altars, firs and flaming brands.*
> —*Aeneid*, Book V, John Dryden, tr.

Every night I sailed a trireme over my breasts, my belly,
made it tack across my bedclothes, all the way to my groin.
Timothy had spent weeks carving a whole fleet,
each balsa ship outfitted with dragon or full-chested lion
to seize the swells in its mouth. I imagined my brother
in his bed also conquering his waves. He'd read enough Vergil
to know nothing valuable lasted, how easy it is to drive
a woman mad, torch even an armada, ruin everything,
rapiuntque focis penetralibus ignem, *furore.*
Mothers couldn't stop themselves any more than fire could.
To be true to the Latin, my brother said we had a duty
to burn our ships too. In the *Aeneid* the rescuing rain falls
almost immediately. *Whole sheets from clouds* *sent.*
In our backyard: no reprieve. No gods rose to spare our fleet.

Venus

Cui mater media sese tulit obvia silva
    —*Aeneid*, Book I

One night our father and Vergil armed his sons and Aeneas
with bows and arrows to track down a mother
all of us liked. Who'd not be on the hunt for immortal parent
especially one with a quiver slung over her shoulder?
Bare were her knees, loose her hair, wantoned *in the wind.*
She smelled like a goddess, *ambrosiaeque comae* *divinum*
Even a confirmed ten-year-old bachelor like my brother
fell for her. I was grateful. Finally, a mother to look out
for him. No harm could come to either of us with Venus
at our side. But as soon as she slipped from behind a tree
to reveal herself, refulgent, she disappeared as mothers do.
Quid natum totiens, crudelis tu quoque, falsis *ludis imaginibus?*
What use is it to reproach someone once they're gone?
Good Romans, we swallowed our hurt and pushed on.

Discus Thrower, Spear Bearer, Apollo

It's okay,
I told the boy who'd just moved next door.
no one's ever home.
It was our lucky day. Every page we turned
in my mother's neglected museum books
had a penis, Hermes
and Hercules apparently having been carved
just for this purpose: to show off
what they'd been endowed with,
the very proportions of which
on a 6- or 7-foot statue
couldn't help but impress second-graders.
The new kid came right back the next day,
apparently he'd discovered one of the perks of moving
onto our street. Only now
he wanted to add a twist:
Shouldn't we be just as naked too?
You go first, I said.
So he posed as Diskobolos. Then Doryphoros.
Then Apollo battling the Centaurs.
He seemed to enjoy being protected by nothing
but skin
the sun peeping through the window found
right away and wouldn't leave alone
as if it were virgin marble.
It's your turn, my new friend said.
He looked as if he'd been hewn
out of light itself.
So I made up my mind then and there:
there needed to be perfection in this world
but shouldn't there also be
someone to keep his composure and his clothes on
and admire that formal beauty?

Tris Notus abreptas in saxa latentia torquet—

Thus while the pious prince his fate bewails,
Fierce Boreas drove against his flying sails,
And rent the sheets; the raging billows rise,
And mount the tossing vessel to the skies.
　　　　　　　—*Aeneid,* Book I, John Dryden, tr.

Two boys play together so often
that when they spend the night at each other's houses
they take baths together too
and sleep in the same small bed.
They take their model boats to the beach and let them drift
to the center of tidal pools,
and the first boy says to the second,
Some day I'll sail a real boat so far away
you will never see me again.

No, you won't, says his friend.
You'll take me with you.

No, I won't! says the first boy.

The two boys are such good friends
that even though the first doesn't have a real boat yet,
the second helps him sew sails
so billowy they take off their clothes
and wrap the Dacron around them and run
to where the land falls away, the one boy hoping
Aeolus will sweep him off the cliff,
the other afraid
he won't be able to fight off the god of winds.

See the lighthouse, the first boy says.

No, his friend says.

Imagine you do, says the boy who wants to sail away
from everyone. *I will, one day. You'll see.*

No, you won't, his friend says.
You wouldn't know what to do without me.
He's right. When they start building

he will be the one who figures out how
to soak and bend and hammer wood
till it agrees to be a boat.
He will be the one who knows what paint and how many coats
to make the hull seaworthy.

I named the boat
so I get to sail it, says his friend.
I will sail it so far beyond the horizon
even my mother and father will forget
what I liked for breakfast.

I'll come with you, says the one boy
putting his hammer away
where it belongs. *You can't leave without me.*

But the other boy is gone.

Fifty Fatal Brides

All in the compass of one mournful night,
Depriv'd their bridegrooms of returning light.
—*Aeneid*, Book X, John Dryden, tr.

Why, about to go into the battle of his life,
did Pallas strap on a belt, heavy
with fifty silver brides etched into it,
each with a knife in her hand
and a smile on her face?
Had he not been able to imagine
his teeth biting the ground
his snowy body skewered?
If you're a *puer speciosus*
and know your father loves you
why gird your waist with women
who dressed for bed with sharpened blades,
a fanciful text to amuse friends?
We knew not to bother a father with questions
he had no interest
in us asking, the first of which was
how did so many women manage
to kill so many husbands
and how did they get away with it
and all in one night, and didn't any of the husbands
cry out and how could they be that stupid
to let their throats be cut? And
why had one of the virgins spared her bridegroom?
And what was a virgin anyway?
If you're young, you don't fall asleep,
you watch the door.
Hadn't my brother too seen the knife
in our mother's hands. More than once.
Sometimes with moonlight
on the blade. If not this night, then the next.

Nate dea, quae nunc animo sententia surgit?

They march obscure; for Venus kindly shrouds
With mists their persons, and involves in clouds,
That, thus unseen, their passage none might stay
Or force to tell the causes of their way.
                    —*Aeneid,* Book I, John Dryden, tr.

Tonight you're a faithful grandson
and your mother spins fog
for you to wear, a shimmering
in which to walk and listen to
your praise till you shake it off
and before a queen stand, stripped
What boy wouldn't envy Aeneas
he could relate till Dido tasted
of Troy and divorced a dead king
glistening future. *Vivo tentat prae*
some lines too lovely for anyone
So this was how to win a woman:
and then you suffer again, like any
who knows he must tell his story

of sea foam
for a cloak
cloud
soldiers singing
with the mist
down to self.
his tragic tale, one
the ashes
for a living,
vertere amore—
to translate.
you suffer,
storyteller
to the end.

O goddess-born! escape by timely flight

—*Aeneid*, Book II, John Dryden, tr.

1

I was always the one with brains
dripping out of my skull. Guts
spilled from my stomach. Speared. Decapitated.
Disemboweled. Not till Vergil
did we realize the many ways one can kill a man.
No glory if a few Rutulians couldn't be butchered
before breakfast.
Because Timothy was almost always Aeneas
I got to be the one in whom he plunged his sword
so deep it came out my other side,
Timothy insisting our games be so real
and me wounded at least enough to secrete a little
actual blood, believable tears
till even he felt sorry for me.

2

Swollen were his feet,
as when the thongs were thrust—
No! I said. Usually, I let my brother do anything
he asked of me—smear my face,
hack off my hair,
turn me into a bloody shroud—
but when he insisted that I be the ghastly Hector
rising from the grave—not
the booty-laden, triumphant son of Priam
but the one so ravaged
there were holes *bored in his feet and hands,*
body blackened with dust—
I refused. So Timothy settled for weighing me down
with chains so I might rise from the dead
and kiss the ashes on his brow
and he might leave me
and walk straight into the burning streets
not able to delay any longer
the work only he could do.

Quid puer Ascanius?

—*Aeneid*, Book III

I

The night before, Vergil led us down
to the underworld, so the next morning I couldn't tell
who was a ghost now
and who living. The building with its huge eye
loomed over us like a Cyclops
and I feared that I'd be swallowed up
if I walked through the first guarded door.
Inside there were hallways of bodies
bent over, emptied of their souls.
Each room smelled the way I imagine Hades
might, a fire left to burn down
to embers. My brother and I sat in chairs so straight
I thought we were being punished
but I wasn't sure
for what. *Say hello to your mother,*
my father said but my lips couldn't remember
how to use air to make words
so I stared at this woman
who seized hold of my arm.
Maybe she'd never let go of me,
I'd be a ghost too. Maybe
when my father went to lead me away
there'd be nothing left for him to hold onto.
For weeks after I did not speak
to my father or brother but floated
in and out of their rooms and opened my mouth
only to breathe.

2

Who is this? my mother asked on the next visit,
gripping my head between her hands
so tight I was afraid
she might be trying to lift my face away
from my shoulders. I turned to my father
but he had other business

to attend to, and my brother was also occupied
at the window searching
the great lawn below, the garden's rows of flowers
tilting their faces as if trying
to be on their best behavior.
My mother kept staring into my eyes
as if I were hiding there
and the only way she could find me
was to grip even more tightly. Pulling free,
I pressed so close to Timothy it'd be hard to tell
there were two of us.
He shook me off the way he might
a leaf from his sleeve.
All color had been drained from my mother
and she looked like someone just rescued
from a burning city. After we hurried
through the first locked door
and then the second,
my brother turned fiercely towards me
as if he hated me now
more than anyone else in the world.
Our father nudged us into the car.
Behind us walls rose so high
we could never hope to scale them.

Her staring eyes with sparkling fury roll

—*Aeneid*, Book VI, John Dryden, tr.

At Phoebi nondum patiens immanis in antro
bacchatur vates, magnum si pectore possit
excussisse deum; tanto magis ille fatigat
os rabidum, fera corda domans, fingitque premendo.
Ostia iamque domus patuere ingentia centum
sponte sua vatisque ferunt responsa per auras
—*Aeneid*, Book VI

Today, Timothy says, *I'll let you be Aeneas*
for a while. And then he puts on an evening gown
our mother has no use for anymore.
He's sewn stars into its black sky.
Now it's up to me to pluck the requisite fruit
off a golden bough for the Sibyl
—my brother!—waiting at the door
to the bottom of the earth
and then I must watch her/him be seized by Apollo
and strain to shake the god
from her breast. My brother, a priestess
older than Africa, proved even stronger
than ever before, but the god *far stronger still*
presses with superior force,
commands entrance
into my brother in his star-strewn dress,
usurps her organs
and inspires her soul.
That Apollo is invisible doesn't matter,
the writhing goes on before my eyes,
his mouth foaming, my brother so deep in the cave
he seems to have forgotten
that there's really no cave,
he's not really being split open
by the god of truth and prophecy,
and by now I am jealous,
I too want to be entered by a god.

By Vulcan laboured, and by Venus brought

> He shakes the pointed spear; and longs to try
> The plaited cuishes on his manly thigh;
> But most admires the shield's mysterious mould,
> And Roman triumphs rising on the gold
> —*Aeneid*, Book VIII, John Dryden, tr.

Having no private income
and needing a birthday present for our father
so maybe he'd forget it was our fault
he was stuck raising us,
we thought what better gift for a dad
who knows passages from the *Aeneid* by heart
than a shield forged by Vulcan.

Luckily our father hadn't got around yet
to throwing away the sheets of tin
our mother had spent hours working into beasts
with five metallic tongues or six legs
or dresses of fire or wind,
her creasing hammer, planishing hammer,
shears and chisels.

And luckily also one of us was good with metal
and not afraid to fire up our mother's soldering iron
and one of us good
at doing what the other told him,
even if it meant fingers burned,
hands cut from etching tools he was too young to use.
By the time my brother and I finished pounding

and pricking, stamping
and snipping, we had a wolf-suckling Romulus
and Remus, Sabine women;
and Tartarus, and Octavian's Triple Triumph
all worked into the metal:
armor so glorious maybe our father would regret
thinking we were a burden

though we knew he'd not stop thinking it.
Afternoons we became Vulcan's apprentices

and hammered out a shield
so finely wrought it gleamed.
If you work anything—tin, marble—diligently enough
the light always seeks it out.

Don't ask me how I know, but I know

Drepani me portus et inlaetabilis ora accipit.
hic pelagi tot tempestatibus actus heu, genitorem,
omnis curae casusque levamen, amitto Anchisen.
hic me, pater optime, fessum Deseris, heu, tantis
—*Aeneid*, Book III

Father's dying, my brother said.
That's why he read Book IV last night.

That's the only way he had
to tell us.

Timothy set the fact before me as a cat might
a dead mouse. My brother knew things

most kids didn't. *What do we do?*
I asked. *Nothing.* Timothy said

as if the worst had already happened
and now he was surprised

how prepared he was. After Father Anchises—
rescued from burning Troy

and having survived Neptune's petulance
but long before the promised shore—

with no warning, expires,
Aeneas walks the beach, wailing.

But not Timothy. Nor would he let me.
It was the first time

my brother slapped me hard enough
to leave a mark. The way truth can.

Long afterwards you reach your hand to your face
and still feel the sting.

Funeral Games, Easter 1951

To honor our father, we dedicated Easter Week   to games
even the founder of Rome might have approved.   We knew
not to believe the hired lady who kept saying,   "Your daddy
will be home soon." Our father took his scotch   straight
and his Vergil! He was no one's *daddy*. We had   no
gymnasium or hippodrome, but we did have a   large backyard

and in it, Monday, boys, stripped to their boxers,   ran faster
than any wind stirred by Aeolus. Tuesday, boys,   naked again
except for their underwear, wrestled to prove   their worth
to my brother, pious Aeneas, bestowing on Jeff N.   a butter plate,
a soap dish for Duncan S. Each day a new boy   granted silver

engraved with our father's name: for Peter L.,   a loving cup,
a platter for Sam. G. All the neighborhood kids   lusted
for trophies not needed by our father, now gone   for good.
Even the light was greedy for something   to polish.
Wednesday: bows and arrows but no doves   to kill
so everyone shot at starlings too lazy   to fly away

and when Cynthia—we'd run out of boys—   hit the mark
and a real bird fell, she took home a goblet   with our father's
name chasing itself around the lip. Next?   Maundy Thursday
my ingenious brother, with no ships handy,   distributed
sleds rigged with sails. One kid pulled, the other   steered

and on the day before Good Friday, we cheered   and cheered
till Ricky C. held in his grasp a silver lady   with wings
and Pam L.—remember, we'd run out of boys—   a liberty bell
that sounded like a buoy. And then, guess what?   That Easter
our father rose, much to our surprise,   out of his car—
not as dead as we'd believed—and insisted,   right away

the loot each child had fairly won   be returned,
and that Sunday, our bicycle baskets, clanging   with pewter
and silver, we took what we had bestowed back   and thus
the whole neighborhood—especially my brother   and I—learned
divine justice must be done, no matter   how fickle.

The First Time I Saw Laocoön Ensnared by the Gods

I couldn't stop staring at the serpent
about to take a bite out of the father's hip
On Laocoön's either side: a boy
also wrapped up in snakes,
though the father seemed too committed to his own pain

to notice his sons, even his eyebrows bulged
with it, the tendons of his neck
as he tried to wrestle free.
Right away I decided which son not to be:

not the one swooning
in the snakes' fatal embrace, head thrown back,
bee-stung lips parted
to drink in his fate, his suffering
already turned rapture now.

No, I'd never be that lovely
slim-hipped marble
boy with dimpled bottom and curled toes,
for whom a butterfly will be named.

Instead, I'd be the one disentangling
himself, and not just
from the snakes, but from father and brother
as if both of them were lethal too:
forever suffering, forever heroic,

the one glancing up at Laocoön with pity
and reproach, as if to say
what did you do, dad, to land us
in this godawful mess?

Seated Scribe with Stylus in Hand

—Egyptian, ca. 2500 BCE

His old man's stomach
        made him look even more
        naked than he was
but because he was in a book
        I could touch him
        all I wanted,
so I kept investigating his belly
        the way I used to
        with certain stones
I needed to curl my hands around,
        something the rain had loved
        as much as I did,
something even I couldn't ruin.
        That's what I needed
        right then:
a man who'd seen the world
        fall apart
        and knew
that when the walls are crumbling
        the best anyone can do
        is write everything down.

III. STUDYING THE

CLASSICS AT FIFTEEN

And there was Nisus in a forest horrid with fern
And intricate with thorn, sending his voice
Before him as he flew...

High Society

Because you disliked Duncan but thought of me
as your best friend

and Duncan disliked you but also thought of me
as his best friend

and because all three of us hated the lifesaving class
our parents had enrolled us in—

Duncan because he wasn't allowed to hide his substantial belly
inside his shirt

you because you weren't sure you wanted to give mouth-to-
mouth to anyone

and I because I got tired of waiting for the tops of girls' bathing suits
to slip off—alas, they never did—

and because all summer we'd done almost everything
our parents had demanded of us

and now was our chance to do something that'd prove
we had lives of our own,

we steered our bikes in the opposite direction of the Red Cross pool
till our legs started pedaling

without our needing to remind them and we sped through towns
as if they were simply doors

that led to the dimmed lights of Satuit Movie Theater and Arvell Shaw,
Barrett Deems, Trummy Young, and Louis Armstrong

blowing out the "High Society Calypso"
while I sat between my two best friends and got to hold the popcorn

we'd paid extra
to slather with butter and sometimes I found Duncan's

hand groping in the popcorn
with mine, sometimes yours, all our fingers mutually sticky

though Grace Kelly didn't care,
because Bing Crosby was crooning to her on his yacht.

I could feel Dunc's broad left shoulder rubbing against mine
as if to remind me once again

who really was my most faithful friend
and your right knee, Ricky,

kept touching my left knee as if we might as well be part
of the same body, and that

was one of the best days of my life though I didn't know it then,
and then our legs took us home.

Fourteen-year-old boys, we certainly didn't hum Cole Porter
as we pumped up one hill and coasted

down another, but I bet Duncan still knows the words to every song
and I hope you do too.

Book Club

To read *The Satyricon* we rigged up a place in the woods
so far behind your house
no one could find us: a fallen tree
turned into a wave-tossed Carthaginian ship
so we could edge out to its prow.
On page 27 Giton is being lent out to Ascyltos
and on page 46 he's naked yet again
after Encolpius has lost him at dice.
By page 104 he's climbing back into his master's bed
smelling of another's honeyed kisses,
and then on page 239, on that ravaged ship—
the wind pawing it even as it was sinking—
to whom does Giton strap his pale,
whiplashed torso, to whom does he turn his face
to be kissed? *Haec ut ego dixi, Giton vestem*
deposuit meaque tunica contectus
exeruit ad osculum caput. And that no envious wave
should pull us apart as we clung
to each other, Giton put his belt around us both
and tied it tight.
And sometimes you were Giton
and you bound yourself fast to me
And sometimes I was Giton
and you were Encolpius
and I flung my arms around you.
If the winds wanted us that desperately
they'd have to take us both.

How Does a Boy Change His Life?

He buys a boat named after a god with wings
on his feet and then he's not Ricky
anymore, but Rick
and old enough to sail an 18-foot full-keel sloop
out towards a lightship
that has no purpose but to blink all night
and warn, *Beware.*
Any minute a rock could rise
out of even the deepest sea.
It doesn't matter that the clouds are so dark
they might have loomed over Troy.
Rick is already sailing past the jetties
straight into the kind of winds you'd expect
when Zeus gets bored and wants to teach mankind
a lesson it'll never forget.
Rick knows what his tight jib is saying.
You're not the boy your father thinks you are.
No voice will outshout Notus and Eurus,
irrepressible winds straight out of the *Aeneid,*
filling the pocket of his sail with late summer storms,
and call this boy back.

Falling in Love with Lorna Dawes

No one else could do the double spiral
                    better, the cobra twist,
          butterfly stitch, Chinese staircase.
It was summer, we'd just discovered weaving
                    gimp
          and girls and boats
and realized our hands
                    had more purposes
          than we'd suspected
and you must've imagined Lorna's fingers
                    curled tight
          around more
than a tiller. I did! Though it was you
                    around whose wrist
          Lorna wrapped
pliable silver and gold.
                    In our seaside town so affluent
          even kids like me belonged
to the yacht club, that's how a boy knew
                    a girl liked him:
          she bestowed on him jewelry
she'd made herself, opal braided in and out
                    of black, lime green
          interwoven with incarnadine orange.
Gimp obeyed Lorna just as jib line
                    and mainsail did.
          No one kept a belly
in a spinnaker the way Lorna could.
                    That's only partly why
          you dumped me
for her. What boy wants a pretty bracelet
                    from another boy?
          Prefers skinny dipping
with someone whose body
                    he already knows
          having wrestled it
to the ground? So there you were

so far out from land
you must've thought
even with my binoculars
I couldn't see
Lorna had nothing on but
the double spiral you had
interwoven
for her
and you had nothing on
but the cobra twist
she had made for you,
robin's egg blue-red braided
with cloud white
yours and hers
threaded in and out of the same sky.
I loved you both.
I wanted you both to die.

Waiting for the Train

O patria, o divum domus Ilium et incluta bello
moenia Dardanidum! quater ipso in limine portae
substitit atque utero sonitum quater arma dedere
— *Aeneid,* Book II

By day's end, tired of my clothes
telling me what I could and could not think,
I had taken off my jacket, unknotted my tie,
and loosened my shirt.
It didn't seem right to be reading Vergil
with a school blazer on.
Perhaps because I was the only one in the train waiting room
who smelled of soap and water,
a man who didn't look all that different
from my father sat down beside me
and asked what I was reading
and didn't laugh when I told him
that I was, at that very instant, shipwrecked
with Aeneas on a deserted shore.
Since I wasn't used to men finding me
of enough interest to listen
to what I had to say, I couldn't stop talking.
Here's what I love about the Aeneid,
I told the complete stranger,
you can know what's going to happen
and that never prevents it
from happening! When the man touched my cheek
his hand was a different temperature
than I'd imagined, and I didn't push him away.
His fingers slid down my face
to my throat, and stayed there
and then for a moment I wanted him to
do whatever he was considering.
Maybe this was the test I'd been waiting to take
all my life. Maybe everything before
had just been a series of subordinate clauses leading to
a simple subject, verb, and direct object and now
I'd never be the same,
the way Troy was never the same.

Tenebris et carcere caeco

Igneus est ollis vigor et caelestis origo
seminibus, quantum non noxia corpora tardant
terrenique hebetant artus moribundaque membra.
—*Aeneid*, Book VI

Because there was no pleasure to be found
quite like that of having a language
only one other person understood,
I sought out a girlfriend who knew immediately
what I meant when I uncrossed my legs,
or scratched my left eyebrow
or wrote in the dust on a windowsill
The body, a noxious burden.
In the green leather notebook she gave me
I copied lines from the *Aeneid*
till I almost believed my hand
hadn't just translated them onto paper
but made the Latin up
neque auras dispiciunt clausae tenebris et carcere caeco.
Souls in a dungeon cannot see the sky.
I knew my mind, that constant plagiarist,
stole everything it liked to pretend
it had invented, but I needed someone next to me in the car
who hated the world as much
as I did and so both of us pressed into the dark
of each other's body as if it was the only place
where we were free to speak.

The Importance of Stigmata: First Love

As soon as her kisses began exploring more
than my face, I grew worried
that any moment she might change her mind
and sink her teeth all the way
into my neck. My nipples?
Soft of my thigh? She wanted inside me
even more, she warned,
than I wanted inside her,
and her fingers were almost savage
with my zipper and then I was nothing
but a body waiting for the torture
it longed for and feared. I couldn't tell
between caress and punishment,
desire and duress, dragged so deep
into the girl I was so determined to love
I didn't believe I'd ever make my way out.
And from then on nothing else mattered
but this pain I needed
to be pleasure, this pleasure I knew
to be pain. Afterwards
I looked at my hands as if they must be different.
I searched for stigmata.
Nothing of import to the world had happened,
but I lay there as if it had.

Loitering Along the Charles River

The careful chief, who never clos'd his eyes,
Himself the rudder holds, the sails supplies.
A choir of Nereids meet him on the flood,
Once his own galleys, hewn from Ida's wood
                    —*Aeneid*, Book X, John Dryden, tr.

After one more day of explaining the digestive system
of a frog and trying to persuade yet another *x*
to equal *y*, and then missing foul shots
I should have sunk, I wouldn't mind,
on my way home,
encountering a few water nymphs,
maybe a choir of Nereids who've swum upstream
from the sea to meet me *on the flood.*
The world could be tolerable
if at least part of the *Aeneid* could come true
and out of the waves rose women
who talked even more intelligently
than dolphins, and once had been pine trees.
Your navy we were. Vergil's even more direct
than Dryden: *Nos sumus, Idaeae sacro de vertice pinus,*
Nunc pelagi nymphae.
That's pure metamorphosized wood talking
in hexameters, trees
once upon a time hewed and hammered into ships,
then set afire by one god
and then rescued by another the only way
the old gods knew to save anyone:
by turning him or her or it into something other
than who they were. That's what I really wanted
at sixteen. To have nymphs in a ring
enclose my ship and with immortal force
nudge my vessel on its fated yet unfathomed course.

Playing with Fire

As when, in summer, welcome winds arise,
The watchful shepherd to the forest flies,
And fires the midmost plants; contagion spreads,
And catching flames infect the neighb'ring heads.
Around the forest flies the furious blast
And all the leafy nation sinks at last
　　　　　　　—*Aeneid*, Book X, John Dryden, tr.

I used to rake up leaves just so I could see the flames
infecting everything. I was a Rutulian
spreading contagion.
At seventeen I resented my father's faith
in me and so did all I could
to make a grand mess of everything he asked.
Saturdays I didn't tidy up the yard,
but mounted an attack, each leaf
deserving to be punished for falling.
I saw to it that Troy burned again
before my eyes, the blaze so high
my family had to rush out, choking, and beg me
to stop, but that just made me
stoke the flames even higher. Throwing themselves
against everyone's good intentions,
the flames lifted *glittering swords*
and *impenetrable shields.*
They were going to set the neighborhood on fire
or die trying.

Ganymede's Hounds before Football Practice

sublimem pedibus rapuit Iovis armiger uncis
longaevi palmas nequiquam ad sidera tendunt
custodes, saevitque canum latratus in auras
                                      —*Aeneid*, Book V

Even by myself in the mirror
in my jockstrap, I knew
I'd never be swept off by any god
with eagle talons. No son of Chronos,
even at his horniest, would be tempted
to part me from my hounds.
No, I'd never be either cupbearer
or catamite, or even
one of that immortal boy's minders, their palms upraised
to the stars, imploring that distant
light to return the terrified lad
entrusted to their care, but, Great Zeus,
let me be one of the boy's loyal hunting dogs,
even the scroungiest one
who, long after his master's been stolen, still barks
and barks at the moon
as if the moon was ever persuaded by anything
sublunar, poet or dog,
and the heavens ever inclined to show mercy
to mortal cries.

'Heus, etiam mensas consumimus?' inquit Iulus

—*Aeneid*, Book VII, David Ferry, tr.

March 5: Elvis Presley discharged from the army
Eisenhower posts 3,500 soldiers to South Vietnam
a one-ton meteorite hits the village of Gao
St. Louis Hawks defeat Minneapolis Lakers 107-106
Eleventh grade boy reads Book VII, Aeneid
—ABC News

Then they feasted on wheat cakes, not sparing even
The broad green leaves the cakes were set upon
In the middle of the *Aeneid*
Vergil and Dryden throw a party
for the Dardanians and for a brief moment
what matters now
is not the dead stripped of their armor
and anointed with oils,
but tables made of cereal, spelt wafers,
woodland forage, soldiers getting a day off and a picnic
where everyone's so hungry
they devour the picnic basket
and for a brief moment it's possible to eat the world
much to the delight of young Ascanius
whose arrow into a tame stag soon would start a war
as apocalyptic as the one
in which my classmate, yet another *puer speciosus*,
two seats in front of me
would be slaughtered. In truth, four wars
would arise to demand my classmates' lives
and then my students' lives
and a plague
would reduce even the most beautiful men to skeletons
before they died and right now another plague
is emptying the streets.
But on March 5, 1960,
I too was with Aeneas's teenage boy Iulus laughing,
Oh! Look! We're eating the tables too!

61

You Are Having the Same Dream Again

You are helping one more boy out of his armor,
a lad who looks remarkably
like the young man you were,
even with the same mole just below the collarbone,
the same little constellation
of scars on his left arm from the flames
he ground out there, as you did at sixteen, needing to
see how much pain you could bear.
Even the lad's slightly stiffening penis leans drunkenly
to one side, as yours still does.
This is not the dream a man your age should have.
You think this
even as you keep on dreaming.
By now the boy is siting up,
looking straight at you as if to say, *What next?*
What next indeed.

IV. READING THE *AENEID* AT SEVENTY-SIX

The end of it all has come. Wherever they went
You've persecuted the Trojans, by land, by sea,
Brought houses down in turmoil and destruction,
Brought grief into the joyousness of weddings.
I forbid you to try anymore. Enough is enough.

—Jupiter to Juno, *Aeneid*, Book XII, David Ferry, tr.

What to Read a Friend You Have Loved Since You Were Six?

Your friend's near death, but so is Lausus
so you keep pushing through Book X
as if, even in his coma, Rick might still savor
each little extravagance Vergil insists on.
Every adjective mourns the son of Mezentius,
that bright tunic his mother wove for him,
its gold mail nothing now
but a flimsy fabric torn by a sword as unrepentant
as cancer. One more minor character
in a great, troubling, and seemingly endless story
crammed with fallen men:
Asbytes, Eumedes, Chloretus, Sybaris, Dares,
Thersilochus, Thymoetus,
the poet meticulously accounting
for each dead Latin as if no one's inconsequential,
everyone deserves a grammar as embroidered
as the cloak Lausus put on before the battle
so he might take it off afterwards and have the air,
solicitous to his wounds.
For now the Fates prepar'd their sharpen'd shears
And lifted high the flaming sword appears.

If Only

If only I hadn't turned away,
when you paraded
in front of me, your penis
prim as a question mark.
If only I'd let my hands answer.
If only I'd buried my face in your neck.
If only I'd welcomed you all the way
into me, into that darkness
of which I have always been ashamed,
and now you are nothing but ashes,
and the man who had loved you
better than I could have
has taken you to the top of a mountain.
Go, he tells the ashes,
Go before I change my mind.

Another Day, Another Long Walk

The five stages of grief? There's only one.

Weeks after your death I still walk every day,
till my legs refuse to go any further
and I'm far enough from home
so I won't get asked yet again how I am doing.
I try not to focus on anything
but my right foot following my left foot's example
of dogged persistence. This afternoon
there's a boy on the riverbank below
so I seek refuge in a stand of trees
that's chosen this particular hill
upon which to grow as tall as they can.
The boy's already begun tugging off his shirt,
pulling it over his head
the way kids sometimes do, as if that's part of the fun
of stripping: getting lost in the dark
of one's clothes. If anyone were to come upon me
lingering in the high oaks,
they might think I've come purposely
to spy on this boy as he unfastens his belt,
falls to the ground, and leans back
as boys do to yank off their pants, red and white boxers
coming off so easily they seem attached
to the jeans. Three mallard ducks,
having just loosened the river from their feathers,
watch even more intently than I do
as the boy persuades his socks to let go of his feet,
and then he's even more naked
than the ducks and far more naked
than the river
that happens to be wearing a few clouds
as well as a flock of willows
and the wind in their boughs. Damn,
this kid's going to slide into the water
as smoothly as a knife.
But then he doesn't. Just arches his back a little,
stretches his hands over his head,
standing, bare-assed and still, by the river
as if that's as good a way as any of spending
the next few minutes of his life.

Fir? Pine? Maple? Make Up Your Mind, Vergil

quaeque ipsa miserrima vidi
et quorum pars magna fui.
                    —*Aeneid*, Book II

Here's how to make class pass quickly.
        Get the whole room ganging up
on the teacher. *You expect us to care*
        about anyone as stupid
as *those Trojan saps? Duped by a horse?*
        First Vergil claims it's woven
out of fir. Then pine. Then maple.
        Why should we believe anything
he or you say? To make a teacher truly squirm
        show no more mercy
than the Greeks did. Keep up the argument till
        he's almost in tears
and long before the bell rings,
        you're heading out the door
smirking. But what if you're the teacher?
        You skip lunch.
Spend the half hour in a banquet hall
        in Carthage,
where everyone, rapt in silence, hearkens
        to pious Aeneas
who now must finish the story
        he started, though even he's not sure
how men that had been made wise
        by suffering
could have been so quickly fooled
        by weepy Sinon and a few snakes
sent by an ill-tempered sea-god.
        Why must a city already ravaged
be ruined even more? The teacher grieves
        for the broad-shouldered boys
galloping off, high-
        fiving and grinning and just
as doomed as any Dardanian.

Vergil before the Oxford Valley Marine Recruiting Office

As of 6/7: 4,424 U.S. military personnel deaths,
460,000 Iraqi excess deaths.
Even the *Aeneid* doesn't have enough lines
to comprehend history's voracious appetite.
But because I can sing "Study War No More"
only so many times, I've come armed
to the Recruiting Arcade today
with the heavy artillery of Dryden's pentameter,
Asius and Acmon; both th' Assaraci;
Young Haemon, and tho' young, resolv'd to die.
Despite my flourescent sign
and paperback copy of the laureate's translation,
I have no illusions
Vergil will dissuade any young man
from trying the video games inside.
How often does a kid get to kill terrorists
in Levittown, Pa., on a rainy Saturday afternoon?
Iam gravis aequabat luctus et mutua Mavors
Funera: caedebant pariter pariterque ruebant
Victores victique. Neque his fuga nota neque illis.
Even Latin's not up to the task
of persuading the young of the perils
of manifest destiny. *Thus...of kind remorse bereft*
He seized his helm, and dragged him with his left;
Then with his right hand, while his neck he wreathed,
Up to the hilt his shining falchion sheathed.
What can Vergil do but record the fatal blow
in language that shows no clemency to friend
or foe? Maybe next week, I'll bring my grandson.
I suspect a nine-year-old might be more persuasive
than Vergil or any statistics we heap up
as barricade: March 2003: 3,977 civilian deaths;
April: 3,438. Amputations: 500 as of 1/3
(Toes and fingers not counted)

When did numbers ever change a young man's mind?
Maybe a leaflet-wielding fourth grader can?
Maybe next week it won't be raining,
at least we'll have the sun
in our faces and on our side.

Radiant Heat

In my waking sleep, Priam's fated daughter
bestowed flaming torches: "Look for Troy in this very spot.
This is your new dwelling place."
            —*Aeneid*, Book V, Edward Collins Bursk, tr.

The house was once pink
The family bought it because it was sold to them
and had a yard just big enough for three kids and maybe a dog
and no bothersome stairs for the mother
and a garage for the father to turn into a workshop
and fix things that got broken
and best of all central air
and floors
heated by serpentine pipes
that pumped water from a little boiler in the kitchen

and men and women gathered on the sidewalk
holding stones
as if that's why hands had fingers
so they could close around something solid and efficient,
something to throw
with enough force to break windows.
A smiling woman went among the families
handing out miniature American flags
just right for waving
and an ice cream truck full of popsicles
provided the kind of music
only ice-cream trucks can in August.

"What did you think when the Myers moved in?"
    "A gun. Now I'll need to find me a gun."

By 2:30 in the afternoon the parade had started
down Daffodil Road to Dahlia to Darkleaf to Deepgreen,
cars slowing down in front of #43
as if something was about to happen there
and everyone had to see for themselves
though the shades were drawn

and no matter how hard they looked
they didn't have the kind of vision that cuts through walls.

And then it was supper time
and someone shouted, "Things are going to happen
and I'm sticking around to see it!"
And later
someone else, "Let's blast it to pieces!"
but no one had thought to bring dynamite
to the small pink house
though they stayed on the lawn
even after the police escorted the two boys, seven and four,
and the father
and mother holding month-old baby Lynda
and the next day

Aurora rose, spreading her pitying light,
And with it bringing back to sight the labors
Of sad mortality, what men have done
And what has been done to them, and what they must do
To mourn.

A Bedtime Story for My Granddaughter

How about a king hounded from his palace
to a river so high there was no way to swim it
while he cradled his infant child.
Trapped between his own mutinous Volsci
and the equally murderous rapids,
Metabus tucked motherless Camilla in baby bunting
he had to weave right then out of cork bark.

Okay, this is not the tale you thought I'd tell
but it's one the poet Vergil believed
we must hear, how a father bound his child tight
to a spear that as a young boy he'd carved
out of tree so hard
the knife could barely make the wood obey its blade,
and then before he let the spear attempt
what no man should have to ask of it
he prayed to the huntress Diana, Latona's dearest daughter,

and then, with his great right hand,
hurled the hewn oak
and the child strapped to its quivering shaft
across waves that kept opening their huge mouths
to swallow whatever they could
and they had an even greater appetite
than the Volsci who liked to fricassee their captives.
Just before Metabus's vengeful subjects could
seize and feast on him
he stripped off his tunic and dove so deep underwater

even the wiliest of rapids couldn't
reach down and snare him,
and when Metabus rose and shook off the cheated river,
lo and behold, there was his child in swaddling
still fastened to the oak shaft
and with the kind of smile kids get

when they wake, as you do sometimes, Sadie,
to find yourself on the other side of sleep
and the father knew right then and there
this child would grow into a woman
no one would ever vanquish,
nothing would ever prove too much for her.

Venus's Prayer for Her Grandson: A Comparative Study of Translations

> *Nil super imperio moveor. Speravimus ista,*
> *dum fortuna fuit. Vincant, quos vincere mavis.*
> *Si nulla est regio Teucris quam det tua coniunx*
> *dura, per eversae, genitor, fumantia Troiae*
> *excidia obtestor: liceat dimittere ab armis*
> *incolumem Ascanium, liceat superesse nepotem.*
> *Aeneas sane ignotis iactetur in undis*
> *et quacumque viam dederit Fortuna sequatur*
> —*Aeneid*, Book X

I beg you, father, by Troy's smoking ruins:
Let me discharge Ascanius from the war
Unharmed—please let my grandson live, Aeneas
Can toss on foreign seas, for all I care;
Whatever road fate grants him, let him follow,
But let me take his son from ruthless battle.

Who wants a goddess for a mother
if she's going to throw her son under the bus
the way Sarah Ruden's Venus does here?
Hadn't pious Aeneas's mom caused enough trouble
using one son to mess with another,
shrinking Cupid down to a facsimile
of Ascanius and making him press his soft lips
to Dido's famished ears and pimp his father?

Ruden's Venus is no feminist. She gets Aeneas fed,
laid, nursed back to fighting shape
for a war that'll cost thousands of mothers' sons
and then has the gall to say, *Aeneas*
Can toss on foreign seas, for all I care.

Dryden's Venus is not much better.
She's ready to cheat her grandson
out of his big chance to make his papa proud:
Inglorious let him live, without a crown.
The father may be cast on coasts unknown,
Struggling with fate; but let me save the son.

David Ferry's translation is determined to rehabilitate
a monster like Ascanius's grandma,
his generous words put into her venereal mouth:
But let me protect this child,
My palaces, Idalia, high Paphos, Amathus, Cythera,
Where he can live out the length of his peaceful life,
Under their sheltering roofs, far from the wars
And all their terrible glories, his armor unused
Beside him where he sits and reads his book.

Here poetry once again manages to disarm a boy
without disgracing him;
young Iulus sits down with a good book
under sheltering roofs.
This Ascanius is not doomed
to an inglorious life, but given a library card.

130 Lowell Avenue

Aerea cui gradibus surgebant limina, nexaeque
aere trabes, foribus cardo stridebat aenis.
Hoc primum in luco nova res oblata timorem
leniit, hic primum Aeneas sperare salutem
ausus, et adflictis melius confidere rebus.
                                        —*Aeneid*, Book I

When I met Keesta for the first time
he was waving to passing cars
from a lawn chair in the small patch of grass
before a house exactly like
the houses on either side of it
and beside him was a rusted red wagon
full of hubcaps for sale, dozens
of silver-spoked circles pulling the sun down to his front yard.
Only I ever called 130 Lowell Avenue
a cottage, its six rooms home
to grandmother, unmarried aunt, widowed uncle,
father, mother, and child,
and cat named Cigar and a bird named Randy.
In the one room that didn't have a bed, toilet, or stove,
I was invited to sit
on the walnut sofa with plaid cushions
beside the walnut end table
and in front of the walnut coffee table,
and I looked up at the Virgin Mary framed on the wall
and was served ginger ale
from the old television set now a liquor cabinet,
and I smelled the baked lasagna
impatient to be devoured in the next room,
and noticed no books except a Bible
that'd obviously not been read in a very long time
and a photo album
full of pictures of a pudgy, bespectacled child
with a smile that seemed to say, *I know*
I'm everyone's darling
but still I must make my own way,
and it was then that, like Aeneas, I first began

to dare to hope that there could be
safety here, and I swore
unlike Aeneas I'd never forsake
this chubby girl who grew into a slender economics major
with a student loan and lovely cheekbones
and whom I'd only just kissed a month ago.
No, I'd do almost anything not to betray her
or anyone in her house.

A Quiz for Those Who May Have Found a Father's Suicide Note

Match the lines to its author/translator. Your choices:

Father

Dryden

Seamus Heaney

Vergil

Sarah Ruden

David Ferry

Son

Not far from here the fields called the Fields
Of Mourning stretch out in all directions.
On these plains, hidden on shadowy paths,
Secluded and embowered in myrtle groves,
Are those who suffered hard and cruel decline
In thrall to an unremitting love.

Nec procul hinc partem fusi monstrantur in omnem
Luguentes Campi; sic illos nomine dicunt.
Hic, quos durus amor crudeli tabe peredit,
secreti celant calles et myrtea circum
silva tegit; curae non ipsa in morte reliquunt

Beyond this but not far, and widely spread,
Are the Fields of Lamentation. That is their name.
Here is where those whom desire has wasted away
Are hidden in secret walkways, in myrtle groves;
They cannot give up their longings even in death.

Not far from thence, the Mournful Fields appear,
So called from lovers that inhabit there.
The souls, whom that unhappy flame invades,
In secret solitude and myrtle shades
Make endless moans, and, pining with desire,
Lament too late their unextinguished fire.

Even though lovers may die, their desires don't.
They seek out secret myrtle, dark paths; shadows
Confer dignity even on lovers who, fueled by self-pity,
Refuse to stop mourning themselves.
Not far from the groves of suicides are the Fields
Of Mourning, are the Fields of Lamentation.

The nearby fields of mourning, as they are called,
Hidden tracks, with myrtle trees around them,
Shelter the victims of cruel, wasting love.
Even in death their passions do not leave them.

Beloved, I shall be true to you long after I die.
Everywhere you are not now is a Field of Lamentations.
There, souls seek out shadows, naked
As the myrtles in which they hide, enthralled
By their desires. The fields of mourning are always close by.

What to Do During a Pandemic

As they did in our great grandmothers' time
the streets patiently wait
for the hearses to cart the dead away.
We wash our hands.
Again and again. We know hands are capable
of ruining lives. They've done it
before. We do trust our legs
and go for long walks.
We walk so far we're not sure
where we are or if we can get back from there.
Then we make it back from there
and are grateful for that small victory at least.
Are we worried more about the contagion
we inhale or the contagion
we exhale? We keep our thoughts
to ourselves. In a time of plague no one wants to hear
what anyone's really thinking,
even before the pandemic, some of us sure
we were already contaminated.
No mask to disguise that.
No deep breaths or walks there and back.
When did the Fates ever change their course
just because someone washed their hands?

One More Book I Had to Blow the Dust Off to Read

Pede tendite, cursumn addite, Encolpius, convolate planta.
...Consumptis versibus suis immundissimo me
basio conspuit....Profluebant
per frontem sudantis acaciae rivi.
I hadn't realized Latin could get me stiff
and sad at the same time.
The translator had left the truly dirty parts
in the original language, but
in the margins: my father's distinct penmanship:
"What soft little fingers, Encolpius,
what flexible bums,"
the old eunuch whispered
as if the words needed to touch me
before his hands did.
And then he straddled me on the couch
and smothered me in his sloppy kisses.
I wanted to be repulsed
but, no, he looked like some cracked wall
standing desolate under a pearly moon.
Each consonant and vowel carved into the page
as if everything my father set his hand to,
even porn, proved marble.
Just inside the front cover, beside my father's signature,
the date told me
he hadn't been that much older than me
when he first opened its pages.
He and I had hard-ons, decades apart?
Just under his name
I wrote my own name and put the date
and returned *The Satyricon* to its high shelf
in my father's study, taking a chance
that if he ever thought to take down Petronius,
my Dad would know I'd been naked
with an aging castrato—and him!—
one rainy September afternoon.

Amitto Anchisen, hic me, pater optime

—*Aeneid,* Book III

Why does the Aeneid *speak to men at sixty*
and boys at twelve? I watch my son swing his hand
inside his son's. Who leads? Who's led?
Vergil before bed. The only way I pray.
I pray for both father and son.

—D. S. Winnicott

First, I unbutton your pajama top
and with one hand slip it up and off your shoulders
and with the other hand,
as lightly as possible, ease you forward
so as not to ask too much of your arms,

and then I undo the cord around your narrow waist
and take you by the ankles
and tilt you up
just enough to slide off your pajama bottoms and your diaper
as I used to with your grandchildren.

Now I sweep your thoroughly resentful body off the bed
and carry you who had Homer
in the Greek and Vergil in the Latin
all the way to the plastic bath chair
where you glower like a deposed emperor

waiting for the humiliation
only lukewarm water and baby shampoo can bring
and because bathtubs are not a place for talking
but for singing
I start the song other sons have probably sung—

You can do it, I know you can do it—
I have your last dream under my wet and soapy hands,
and all the longings that carried you
in and out of boardrooms and whores' arms
and drunk tanks and libraries full of your own books.

Afterwards I rinse you off
and dab every hollow and crevice in you

that needs comfort
and I dress you in what still smells of the clothesline's breezes
and button your shirt

as if getting you ready to receive royalty
and I kiss your forehead
partly, I admit, in revenge,
against you who never kissed me willingly
and partly in adoration

for you who faced Cyclopes and Sirens far worse than me
and primarily in wonder at the indomitable brow
that still holds behind it
Aristotle and Hesiod, Sophocles and Petronius too.
Even as I lift my lips away

and turn off all the lights but one
I refuse to imagine
you'll ever leave us as Anchises had to leave weary Aeneas
who'd rescued him from their burning home.
And for what? the son wondered

as he buried his father on the shore
from which he must set sail,
this final trial a father can ask of a son
And soon, Πατέρας,
the gods will drive me from this place.

The Procession to the Palace of King Neptune

"Say, I intreat thee, what achievement high
Is in this restless world, for me reserv'd.
What if from thee my wandering feet had swerv'd,
Had we both perish'd?"—"Look," the sage replied...
Endymion, with quick hand, the charm applied—
The nymph arose, he left them to their joy,
And onward went upon his high employ,
Showering those powerful fragments on the dead.
And, as he pass'd, each lifted up its head,
As doth a flower at Apollo's touch.
Death felt it to its inwards: 'twas too much.
                                                    —*Endymion*, Book III

How could a man, barnacled as rock
at low tide, rank as seaweed,
have a story worth listening to
by a prince enamored of the moon?
And yet Endymion finally took the wand
and scroll from Glaucus's knobby fingers
and did as he was told:
tore the parchment into *pieces small as snow*,
and *struck the wand against the empty air*
times nine, and a host of lovers lifted their heads
as if the sun himself had descended
to wake each of the dead
and, no matter what they had suffered,
each shook off a thousand years of *imprison'd sleep*,
and Endymion and Glaucus led this multitude revived
and limber again, jubilant,
down marble steps, *pouring as easily*
as hour-glass sand, toward *jasper pillars* and *opal domes—*
'tis dizziness to think of it!—
and all I have to do now is keep reading
till my own resurrected dead march with them
as if they too had sailed in the *same capsiz'd ship*
and been locked forever
in the anonymity of a sleep so sound
no words could rise from them
to our expectant ears. There's David Kime laughing
his Woody Woodpecker laugh

as if he'd never been consumed in flames,
and Sandy Becker next to him,
so distracted by a heron
she forgets to bring that gun to her mouth,
and Doug Hughes trails behind
not quite believing his good luck
at having his body back again
and Doris Sivel holds a book she'd been putting off
reading, and Barbara Winne, her back
finally straight again, takes notes
on the most common of flowers since everything now
seems exotic, and Del Purscell's there too
putting the world straight
once more, and Nils Falk has a list
of questions for King Neptune because he can't return
to his wife empty-handed—
that'd make dying a complete waste—
and Pamela Perkins-Frederick and Herb Perkins-Frederick
in their matching neon green hoodies
have already cornered Triton
to discuss the thermodynamics of waves,
and Robert Fraser leads the way with his walking stick
for a whole legion of minor, minor poets
because all of us have been raised from the dead
but that doesn't mean
we don't need a little help still keeping our balance
on the golden steps
in the marble halls to which Endymion had led us,
especially if we were singing,
and by now who of us isn't singing?

ACKNOWLEDGMENTS

With deep gratitude:

to John Timpane for his attentive reading;

to Ragged Sky Press for publishing this, my final book of poetry, and to Ellen Foos for her generous and careful editing, and to Jean Foos for her book design;

to Deborah Kahn for her cover painting *Green Animal with Figures;*

to the Spring Poetry workshop community for inspiring me with your commitment to poetry;

to my friends George Drew and Helen Lawton Wilson for their years of encouragement;

to Brandi George, Lisa Fay Coutley, and Lorraine Henrie Lins who read this book in manuscript and believed in it;

to *Palette* for publishing "For the Boy I Wanted, Fifty Years Ago, to Take to the Senior Prom;"

to John Dryden, David Ferry, Seamus Heaney, Sarah Ruden, whose translations of the *Aeneid* make it come alive on the page so that we grieve for Creusa and Dido, Palinurus and Pallas, Nisus and Euryalus, and even savage Turnus and pious Aeneas. Thanks also to Michael Heseltine's 1913 translation of the *Satyricon;*

to my very own Achates, whom I buried in 1990 but who lives in that same world Aeneas visited in Book VI. Pam is there too, and Herb and Sandy and David and Jonathan, Jerry and Chip, Katherine and Keesta, Catherine and Liz. And Rick.

> *In tears as he speaks, Aeneas loosens out sail.*
> —*Aeneid*, Book VI, Seamus Heaney, tr.

Born on the same day as Shakespeare, CHRISTOPHER BURSK has no illusions he is Prospero breaking his wand, though this is his final book of poetry. A recipient of PEW, NEA, and Guggenheim Fellowships and author of eighteen books, he is grateful to have had his writing recognized by The AWP Donald Hall Poetry Prize, the Allen Ginsberg Prize, the Green Rose Prize, the Patterson Prize, Bellingham Review's 49th Parallel Awards, the New Letters Prize in Poetry, and the Milt Kessler Book Award. Most importantly, he is the proud grandfather of six.